Come to Me

JOANNA M. WILLS

LUCIDBOOKS

Come To Me

Copyright © 2022 by Joanna M. Wills

Published by Lucid Books in Houston, TX
www.LucidBooks.com

eISBN: 978-1-63296-550-9
ISBN: 978-1-63296-549-3

Table of Contents

I'd like to express my deepest thanks to my friend, Marnie Piuze, for your selfless support, encouragement, insightful contributions and prayer covering. I am eternally grateful for you. My gratitude to my daughter, Jessika Packman, for your loving nudges over the years encouraging me to write. Many thanks to all who supported me in prayer, especially my dear friend, Cynthia Esters. Thank you to my son, Justin Wills, for your love and support. Many thanks to the incredible team at Lucid Books for your steadfastness and expertise to bring these pages to print. From the depths of my heart, I thank my Lord Jesus for your unfailing love and the sweet flow of your Spirit in writing this book.

Introduction

When I was a young believer, I spent years struggling with respiratory illnesses. Along with this, my 1st child suffered from colic and I felt helpless in my ability to calm her and ease her pain. It was through these trials that I found my heart leaning into Jesus. One thing I remember well is rocking my crying baby girl feeling helpless and hopeless and I began to sing to Jesus, seeking Him. As I sang, I felt my heart turning, looking for Him and peace began to permeate my being dissipating my anxiety. There in my rocking chair, I entered the presence of the Lord, and as that happened my baby girl stopped crying and fell asleep.

I had been in desperate need having nothing left in myself and I came to Jesus just as I was. That was the beginning of my experiential realization that I could truly come to Jesus regardless of my inner state of being or my circumstances. It was also the beginning of my understanding that all He requires from us is simply a turning heart, a coming to Him for Himself, and all we need is found there in Him.

I wrote this book with a desire to share my experiences and my insights in order to inspire and encourage anyone and everyone to come to Jesus. Whether you are just beginning your life with Jesus or you've been with Him for many years, or if you have always believed but never found the sweet intimacy His presence brings, come just as you are and seek to live a life in the simplicity of coming to Him. Come not just once, but through all the days of your life embarking upon a journey into God Himself.

I too am on this journey daily. Let's step out together answering Jesus's call, "come to Me." He is patiently waiting for our turning hearts so that He can make His presence known.

One

The more I go on with the Lord the less I know. When I was a young Christian I thought I knew so much. I was in a church where the Word was alive, full of revelatory light and the Spirit was free-flowing. I felt like I was constantly being lifted to another realm where revelation upon revelation excited me and compelled me to abandon all and surrender my heart and life to Jesus completely. I often prayed to become an overcomer and I desired to know Jesus as John, Peter, and Paul did. I gave myself to the church, to serve wherever I could and I was radical trying not to compromise with the world or with religion. I thought I was on fire for the Lord and perhaps I was to some degree but looking back, I reflect on a high level of my own soulish power and fire. I smile with gratitude in the reflection because I believe the Lord knew my heart and that is what matters to Him. Now, more than 50 years later, it seems that all I really know is that I don't know my Lord Jesus enough. I may have been given much revelation but experientially it boils down to one simple thing - I must answer his call, "Come to Me," day after day, hour after hour, moment by moment. It is an intimate call that ushers us into the limitless love and unity of the blessed Trinity and the knowledge of God. And out of that, out of Him, the true Christian life flows.

Over these years and to this very day, I am continually impressed at the simplicity and yet the depth of the word "come." The disciples began their journey, their calling, by responding to Jesus saying to them, "Come, follow me…" (Matt 4:19[a] NIV) His call to come and follow Him first and foremost had to be responded to. If they didn't simply come to Him and follow Him, they would have missed out on becoming a friend of the living God Himself and they would have missed out on witnessing the wonders of the coming Kingdom in action on the earth in that very day. They would have missed out on knowing Jesus, the Son of God and the

Son of man. I could go on and on, but simply put, they would have missed out on all that God had for them.

Jesus never demands that we come to Him. His invitation to us to come allows us the choice to respond or not to respond. I think most of us want to come to Him but the things of our own lives and our desires often keep us and hold us back. Jesus, the Lord, in patience waits. He waits for our hearts and our will to line up to answer His call. That is when we can come to Him in simplicity and purity.

We are no different than the disciples, other than the times we were born into. Today Jesus continues to call us to Himself. The more we respond and come to Him with an open heart, the more we want to keep coming to Him. The more we come to Him the more we will be like the apostles who discovered not only who He is but they also came to know and experience His incomparable love and power.

No matter how well our day is or is not going, Jesus calls us to come to Him. Him, in whom all things exist and are held up. Him, who sees all things, knows all things. Him, who is light and life. Him, who is the be-ginning and the end. Him, who called us before He knit us together in our mother's womb. Him, who knows the number of hairs on our head. Him, who loves us and shed His blood for us. Him, who quenches our deep-est thirst and satisfies our hunger. Him, who heals our wounds and gives rest to our souls. Him, who was and is and is to come. Simply come with an open heart, that is all He asks and He'll do the rest.

Two

No one who truly seeks to know God desires to be locked up in religious prison bars. I was a devout Catholic growing up. At different stages of those years, I did all I could to be a "good" Catholic – rosary praying, novenas, weekly visits to the confessional, strict obedience to Lent restrictions, and even Mass before school during some of my High School years. But there was always a hidden questioning in my heart and a desire for something more.

I began to seek my own understanding of God and to sort out my religious beliefs in college, as many college students do. It was a turbulent time because it was the late 60s and my generation was questioning everything. I'm sure you know all about the Hippies, and yes, I was one. I was more of a passive conformist taking on the persona of the "love child", as opposed to the outspoken activists. I was deeply introspective as I observed what was going on and I tried to understand the great changes that were happening. My religious learning shook in the quake of overturned morality; as did my learning to respect authority in the defiance of it.

I began to question God. Admitting to myself that after all the years of doing the right thing I was empty and unsatisfied, I looked around and I saw a great lack in the religious. I shunned Christianity and questioned God's very existence not having the maturity to see that religion and its forms were the problems. I remember talking to God telling Him I didn't think He existed and asking if He does exist, who is He? No answer came and I continued my life putting my struggle with God aside. I identified myself as an agnostic trying to embrace the times and the life fully.

I got a bit lost in the upheaval and entrapped by the lightheartedness I found by smoking marijuana and hashish. I lived daily in an undercurrent of depression and every day that I wasn't high I got more and more depressed. Suicide became a constant thought and in my free time, I'd often find myself standing on an overpass looking down on the traffic as I contemplated if I could actually jump. Other days I'd think about how I could end my life.

Depressed and emotionally dependent on marijuana for happiness and escape from the seemingly bleak truth of the futility of man's existence, I resorted to attempting suicide by taking pills. It was that day in 1969 that God chose to visit me. As I lay on my bed in a corner of my room, the room suddenly filled with a "presence" which caused me to sit up. I could almost visibly see this presence and I pushed back into the corner of the walls, knees to chest. I wasn't afraid because peace like I'd never known, overtook me. This presence filled the room floor to ceiling, except for the small space where I sat.

We did not speak to one another audibly, but I knew this was God. There was an internal revelation that I later could not dispute. I simply knew without a doubt, from the deepest part of my being, that God was in my room. He was speaking to me, loving me, letting me know He does exist, and giving me hope. I don't know how long He was there, but when His presence left as suddenly as it had come, I was not dead nor did the pills I had taken have any effect on my body.

I got off the bed and grabbed my journal to write. As I sat down I sensed a small, faintly visible white dove on my shoulder, an added confirmation that God had been there. At that moment I knew I had to find out who God is. I remember I said out loud, "You are real, but who are you, God?" I did not hear an answer but from that deep place within me, I was overtaken with a desire to step out and seek Him. I believe this was the first call I heard internally, "Come to Me."

Three

After such a revelatory experience I put all my energy into finding out who God is. I spent several months looking into "God avenues" seeking that presence that would identify the One who had visited me and saved my life for a reason. The eastern religions were very popular at the time so I did a lot of reading about each and asked a lot of questions of my peers. I decided to follow the Zen Buddhist teachings and I began eating a Zen macrobiotic diet which was presented as a means of achieving spiritual unity and an enlightened state of being through food and Zen principles. I chewed each mouthful of my food 100 times and adhered to the strictness of the food preparation as I tried to live in the moment seeking spiritual enlightenment.

After some time, I began to wonder if I'd ever reach nirvana even with trying so diligently to do all that was required. During this time of deeper reflection one of my close friends, Josh (pseudonym), had a visit from one of his friends, Lucy (pseudonym), who lived in California. Josh and I sat and listened to Lucy as she talked about the "Lord" without saying who this Lord was. Her exuberance captivated me but it wasn't so much what she said that held my attention but rather how joyful and full of light she was. Something deep within me identified what I saw in this young woman as similar to the sense I had when I sat in God's presence.

I wanted to know Lucy's Lord. After she went back to California Josh and I decided we would visit Lucy and look into what she had found. Several months later we packed up and set out on our cross-country excursion with hope and expectation.

Soon after our arrival in California Lucy took us to an international conference that was being held in a huge auditorium of an old hotel. We walked into a boisterous crowd of people full of joy. I remember smiling with wonder as we found seats in the balcony and as I looked down at the stage, I saw a full-length banner hanging above it stating, "Christ vs Religion." I remember being somewhat in awe at such a bold statement and then people began to get up in sections calling on the name of Jesus in their own language. As I listened my heart responded and I knew without a doubt that this was the same presence of God that was in my room that day of visitation.

And there in that place, as the name of Jesus bellowed around me in many languages the "presence" overtook me and I immediately knew God is Jesus. I suddenly was with the one, Jesus, who I spoke to as a child and my thought at that moment was, "it is you, my old friend, Jesus!" Jesus, the one I talked to as I sat in a tree I had climbed. The one whose love I felt when I hugged a tree trunk. Jesus, the one who the beauties of nature caused me to look for in the heavens. There I stood enveloped by Him and I was happy, so very happy.

A few days later I had an incredible water baptism that brought about the baptism of the Spirit. I saw the heavens open right through the ceiling over the stage of the hotel where the baptismal pool sat. I could "see" what my natural eye could not and I began to praise God over and over with shouts of joy. That deep call within to "come" led me to seek and that day, with all my heart and mind, I consecrated myself to the Lord God, Jesus, and His eternal purpose.

Sometime later I looked back on Lucy's visit and our conversation about a Lord she didn't name. In my reflection, I realized the wisdom of God is always at work to draw us to Jesus. Josh and I were adamantly against Christianity at that time and I'm not so sure we would have set out across the country to explore the reality of Jesus had Lucy named Him at her visit. Lucy told me she had been ashamed that she had not told us that it was Jesus she spoke of but I assured her that God's wisdom was working through her as He drew Josh and me to seek further. God knows each one of us and in His love and gentleness He patiently and intelligently works to draw us to Jesus with open hearts to hear His call, "come to Me."

I had put Jesus on the shelf with religion, but He stayed with me through all my turmoil and seeking. He visited me at just the right moment in time and He brought me to people who knew Him, had real joy and relationship with Him, and where I could recognize Him as the One who had visited me in my room. Now I knew who God was. My knowing was that same internal knowing I had in His presence that day in my room. As I began to call on the name of Jesus out loud with a heart turning to see Him, I found the simplest yet most profound way to come to Him. It was the beginning of an intimate relationship, my spiritual eyes seeing Him and my spiritual ears opened to hear His voice, "Come to Me."

Four

I do not doubt that even before we receive Jesus as our savior, He is at work in all the stuff of our lives, both the positive and the negative. He knows our hearts and our minds and He uses everything to ready us to acknowledge His call and open our hearts.

Some people make choices that result in hardening their hearts, but often other people's choices cause us pain and suffering which can be the basis of a hardened heart. I had a combination of both. My home environment as a child was filled with turmoil that affected me deeply. And as I've already acknowledged, my choices in my college years were often very unhealthy. All these things eventually contributed to the hardening of my heart to God. My heart was blanketed with symptoms of depression and loss of hope. Years later, on the brink of suicide, my heart finally let down its guards and opened. In came the presence of God at the moment He knew I would respond to Him, acknowledge Him, and allow Him to touch my wounds. In the years following He revealed to me how very much His hand was on me through it all.

God will draw us to Jesus but we must exercise our free will to decide to seek, to come. When I look back on that visitation in my room, I realize that my need to find out who God was, actually originated from that call deep within me, drawing me to choose to step out and find Him. His visitation was the opening of the door drawing me to seek Him, to come to Him, and by His mercy, I stepped through the door.

The choice to seek Him is not a one-time decision. It is up to me to choose to come to Him daily. Yes, He lives in me, but my choice remains to turn my heart to Him, to come to Him, or to continue in my own strength, my own self. Over the years I chose all too often to continue in my own strength and understanding or to look to other people for answers and help, but year after year, day after day I eventually learned to quickly come to Him, just Him. David's proclamation in Ps 16:11 has become my reality, "You will show me the path of life; In Your presence is fullness of joy; At Your right hand are pleasures forevermore." (NKJV)

I learned much from David in his Psalms. He came to the Lord just as he was, with no pretense, no religious forms. He laid all his thoughts and emotions, his fears and his disappointments, his desires, and even his failures before the Lord but always with a heart turning toward God. He talked intimately with God as a friend. The end result most often was praise, thankfulness, and worship. I truly believe that David, coming in honesty, found himself in God's presence where he could see Him with his spiritual eyes. A place where everything else fell away and no longer held him captive. I can be bold to assume this because it is my own experience in coming to Jesus in my daily life.

David seems to have lived wholeheartedly in response to this call to come. His passion appears to have consumed him and even when he failed and sinned gravely, he didn't close his ears or his heart and so, even soiled by shedding the blood of another man to take his wife, he chose to respond to the call to come. There in God's presence true repentance humbled him.

David knew God's unfailing love and His compassion that releases forgiveness for the repentant heart so he could come in confidence even after committing adultery and murder. Psalm 51(NIV) is his prayer of repentance. "Have mercy on me, O God, according to your unfailing love; according to your great compassion blot out my transgressions. (v1) … Against you, you only, have I sinned (v4ª) … Open my lips, Lord, and my mouth will declare your praise." (v15)

God described David as a man after His own heart. He was a man who found the simplicity of coming just as he was and there in God's presence, he continually learned to know God more and to know God's heart desires. In essence, David was letting go of his thoughts, feelings, desires, and will before the Lord who is light and life. All that held him captive now faded and dissipated so that he could see the One he was coming to. There in His presence, David experienced the living

God and his heart was humbled to absolute surrender to God Himself.

Five

God's desire has always been for us to come to Him. In Isaiah, He speaks to all who will hear, "Come, all you who are thirsty, come to the waters; and you who have no money, come, buy and eat! Come, buy wine and milk without money and without cost ... Give ear and come to me; listen, that you may live." 55: 1 & 3ᵃ (NIV) Jesus spoke a similar word in the gospel of Matthew, "Come to me, all you who are weary and burdened, and I will give you rest." 11:28 (NIV) It seems so simple, so easy – just come.

So why do we often forget to be so simple? Oswald Chambers attributes the stubbornness of our hearts as an obstacle to the simple childlike response to come to Jesus. He says, "The attitude necessary for you to come to Him is one where your will has made the determination to let go of everything and deliberately commit it all to Him."[1]

The cares of this life often easily entangle us and cloud our hearts and minds making it difficult for us to lay the cares down. Often the pain of life with its wounds, abuses, offenses, and losses become the focal point keeping our hearts bound. Other times our inability to forgive traps us and holds us captive. These are just some of the reasons and I list them to help us realize our need for the admonition that Paul spoke to the Corinthians, "But [now] I am fearful, lest that even as the serpent beguiled Eve by his cunning, so your minds may be corrupted *and* seduced from wholehearted *and* sincere *and* pure devotion to Christ." 2 Corinthians 11:3 (AMPC)

Although Paul was warning these believers against being deceived by an antichrist spirit or another gospel than the gospel they received in Christ, over the years I have

---

1   Oswald Chambers, *My Utmost for His Highest: An Updated Edition in Today's Language*, ed. James G. Reimann (Grand Rapids: Discovery House Publishers, 1963), PN.

found that my mind and emotions can create a deception that triggers my will to keep me from simply coming to Jesus with a seeking heart. My will takes the lead to hold me back and I choose to hold onto the thoughts and emotions that have entrapped me. I choose my right to myself. The will must resolutely let go by making a definite choice to turn from myself to Him.

When I first started to pray over this verse asking that I be kept from such beguiling deception, I realized it applies to my heart every day of my life. Satan uses all his subtleness to waylay us through our thoughts and emotions. This self-deception can sound like, "I'm not enough," "I failed again," "I can't do this, it's too hard," "God doesn't love me," "I'm hopeless," "I'll never be as spiritual as….," on and on the lies go. They can also be about the right to ourselves, "I have a right to be - angry, hurt, offended" etc. When our minds are engaged like this our hearts get stuck too and coming to Jesus doesn't seem to be simple.

We can all get distracted from simply coming to Jesus by thoughts, emotions, and circumstances. In Matthew 14:28-30 we see Peter stepping out of the boat in the storm to answer the Lord's call, "come." With eyes fixed on Jesus, Peter found himself walking on water. He was indeed coming to Jesus but then the boisterous wind distracted him and caused him to look away from Jesus. His eyes fixed on the surrounding storm and his mind and emotions were ambushed by fear. You know the story; he began to sink.

To come to Jesus in simplicity and purity we must be willing to allow the eyes of our hearts to get fixed on Him. One of the best passages that has helped my heart to open and to turn is David's prayer in Psalm 139:23-24a, "Search me, God, and know my heart; Put me to the test and know my anxious thoughts; And see if there is any hurtful way in me …" (NASB) Clearly, such a prayer presents a heart humbled before God and a mind willing to lay down all interfering thoughts. The hurtful way is also translated in other versions as a wicked or offensive way. The mind, emotions, and will all affect the heart and its ability to turn. I can't count the number of days in my life that my coming to Jesus has begun with this simple yet weighty request of David's.

Oswald Chambers writes about the importance of letting nothing come between us and Jesus. "Never allow anything that divides or destroys the oneness of your life with Christ to remain in your life without facing it. … Nothing is as important as staying right spiritually. And the only solution is a very simple one- 'Come to Me …' The intellectual, moral, and spiritual depth of our reality as a person is tested and measured by these words. Yet in every detail of our lives where we are found not to be real, we would rather dispute the findings than come to Jesus."[2]

Like David, we can choose to maintain a willingness to allow God to examine our hearts and show us what is in our souls that keep us separated from Him. We come to Him ready to be honest, eager to be corrected, and willing to change so that we can be one with Him. Everything must fade to the background so nothing can obscure our sight and hold us captive. The Psalms that David wrote reveal such a heart over and over again.

2   Oswald Chambers, *My Utmost for His Highest: An Updated Edition in Today's Language*, ed. James G. Reimann (Grand Rapids: Discovery House Publishers, 1963), PN.

The man after God's own heart held nothing back in his own heart and he was quick to repent. He always sought the Lord Himself, seeking His face.

Just as we must turn our hearts to Jesus in prayer and conversation, we can do the same as we open the bible, letting the black and white letters get into our hearts and become life and light to us. When we come to the Word in this way we are coming to Jesus.

David's psalms show that he knew the Word of God was a living way to come to God Himself. The law to him was more than rules to be followed. In seeking to know God and to do His will he leaned into the truth which always lifted him higher, out of himself and out of circumstances. David let the written law get into his heart through meditation and prayer and there before His God the law became alive as the law of life within him and became his delight. Psalm 1:2, "But his delight is in the law of the Lord, and in His law he meditates day and night." (NKJV)

John tells us clearly in the first chapter of his book that Jesus is the Word. "In the beginning was the Word, and

the Word was with God, and the Word was God. …
And the Word became flesh and dwelt among us, and
we beheld His glory, the glory as of the only begotten of
the Father, full of grace and truth." John 1:1, 14 (NKJV)
We too can behold the glory of Jesus Christ when we
seek to come to Him through the written Word.

Six

The apostle John has always been a great inspiration and example for me. He described himself as the disciple Jesus loved. When I first read that I was amazed at the certainty of his statement. There was no doubt in him, that Jesus loved him. As I began to receive a revelation of the intimacy John had with Jesus, I understood why he was so sure of Jesus' love for him. John was like David, he came to Jesus in simplicity and purity, leaned on His breast, and got to know His heart.

I love the old hymn, Just As I Am. Every stanza begins with, "Just as I am," and ends with "O Lamb of God I come." The verses of the song beautifully state the simplicity of coming to Jesus. We see we can come simply because of His shed blood and that He calls us to come just as we are without trying to fix ourselves. No matter how we feel or don't feel or what we have done or what we have not done, there is no other requirement. We can come knowing He will receive us and that He will cleanse us no matter what. We can come knowing He will break down all barriers between us. What more can be said? He simply desires us to come to Him like little children in honest openness.

In the gospels we see that Jesus rebuked the disciples for trying to hinder the little children from coming to Him, telling them that the kingdom of God belongs to such as these, the little children.

Think about how simply and lovingly little children come to their parents. First and foremost, they come sure of the parent's love for them. They come trusting the parent will protect and take care of them and fix their wounds. They come believing the parent can do anything and everything. Children also come to their parents with great joy to show them little things they found, to tell them their hopes and dreams, and they come with excitement over good things that happened to them. They come with laughter and glee and not only when they're in need or fearful.

Oh, that we would not lose such simplicity and surety of the love of God in Christ Jesus for us. Day in and day out His call is always, "Come to Me." When we choose to respond and come, intimacy increases and changes us, transforming us into the image He created us to be, the image of the living God. That intimacy and that transformation set us free from the bondage of a fallen world and the fallen self we inherited from Adam.

In his book, The Attributes of God, Volume 1, A.W. Tozer writes about hearts that come to God simply and for nothing else but knowing Him. "These people want the spiritual experience that comes from knowing God for Himself."[3] He goes on further to say, "And so God takes great pleasure in having helpless people come to Him simply and plainly and intimately. He wants us to come without all that great overloading of theology. He wants us to come as simply and as plainly as a little

---

3   W. A. Tozer, *The Attributes of God Volume 1 with Study Guide* (Chicago: WingSpread Publishers, 2007), PN.

child. And if the Holy Spirit touches you, you'll come like that."[4]

---

4   W. A. Tozer, *The Attributes of God Volume 1 with Study Guide* (Chicago: WingSpread Publishers, 2007), PN.

Seven

You may be wondering how you, an adult, can now become like a child and find the way to simply come. If you reread the quote from Tozer in the previous chapter you will see that he gives us a key, "… if the Holy Spirit touches you, you'll come like that." Ah yes, the third person of the Trinity now takes center stage.

When Jesus told the disciples He must go to the Father, He told them He would ask the Father to send them another Comforter, a Counselor, the Holy Spirit. We can read His words in John's record, "And I will ask the Father and he will give you another Savior, the Holy Spirit of Truth, who will be to you a friend just like me—and he will never leave you. … you know him intimately because he remains with you and will live inside you."

John 14:16-17 (TPT) Jesus went on, "Loving me empowers you to obey my word. And my Father will love you so deeply that we will come to you and make you our dwelling place." John 14:23(TPT)

Jesus went on to describe what the Spirit of God in us will do. "But when the Father sends the Spirit of Holiness, the One like me who sets you free, he will teach you all things in my name. And he will inspire you to remember every word that I've told you." John 14:26 (TPT) John reiterates this in 1 John 2:27 saying, "But as for you, the anointing (the sacred appointment, the unction) which you received from Him abides [permanently] in you; [so] then you have no need that anyone should instruct you. But just as His anointing teaches you concerning everything and is true and is no falsehood, so you must abide in (live in, never depart from) Him [being rooted in Him, knit to Him], just as [His anointing] has taught you [to do]." (AMPC)

So, this wonderful Holy Spirit, the very Anointed One who comes into us, is the One who touches us. His touch stirs us, guides us, and leads us to Jesus in simplicity. All that is asked of us is that we respond by turning our hearts to Jesus, which is the essence of our "coming" to Him.

Referring to the heart, 2 Corinthians 3:16 says, "But the moment one turns to the Lord with an open heart, the veil is lifted *and they see*." (TPT) We see Jesus as the way, the truth, the life, and like little children we just want to be with Him. In my experience, the more I turn the more I want to turn. I become increasingly sensitive to the Holy Spirit's impulses and find "coming" becomes my way of life.

This sensitivity and seeing is a process and is closely connected to the surrender of our will to Jesus. I can recall many times in my earlier walk with Jesus when turning to Him wasn't so easy. I might have been over-wrought with difficult circumstances, offenses, or any other thoughts and emotions. I would call to Jesus but my heart didn't want to let go of whatever emotion or thought was connected to the external or internal things bogging me down. I sometimes stubbornly dug my heels in not wanting anything but my own way. I kept my eyes focused on myself instead of allowing my heart to turn away, completely away, to seek the face of Jesus.

It is often because of pain, discomfort, or desperation that we finally allow the Holy Spirit to lead us to Jesus. Earlier I described how in desperation for my colicky child and my inadequacy to alleviate her pain I found how to simply come to Jesus. At that time, I was desperate and the Holy Spirit was able to guide my heart to turn away from the problem and into the presence of Jesus.

What I had to learn going forward was that daily life (both the good and bad of it), life's circumstances, my own will, and even my desires often get in the way. There were so many lessons over the years that worked to reveal this to me by shedding light on my unconscious mindset. This mindset dictated that I had a right to myself and to all that I was feeling, thinking, and desiring.

For example, if someone offended me and I began to let that offense take ground in my heart, the Holy Spirit would prompt me to turn my heart. But the eyes of my heart stayed fixed on the offense and my "right" to feel it, so there could be no real coming to Jesus. I was stuck in the offense and even more so in my right to hold onto it.

Little by little I began to understand that I had to include my will, the surrender of it, to come to Jesus. I had to learn to exercise my will to let go of my offense by handing it over to Jesus while I turned my heart to Him. I learned from David's writings to tell my soul to be still, allowing my spirit to follow the Holy Spirit straight to Jesus. There, in His presence, I no longer held or was held by the offense. The offense dissipated in His presence and love took its place while forgiveness toward the offender rose in my heart. More and more through these experiences, I saw more of who Jesus is and my way became one of coming to know and desire Him above all else.

Eight

So, we turn our hearts and come to Jesus. Then what? As I said, we see Jesus and that is something big in itself, but there is more. 1 Corinthians 6:17 highlights a unity that belongs to us when Jesus comes into our hearts as Lord and Savior, "But he who is joined to the Lord is one spirit with Him." (NKJV) Jesus doesn't live in the believer separate, alone. He becomes joined to the believer in his/her human spirit. Every time we respond to the influence of the Holy Spirit and turn, we connect to that unity. The more we yield to the impulses of the Holy Spirit the more we live in the power of that unity.

Coming to Jesus is coming to all that He is and has. All that He is and has is ours through the One He has sent to us, the Holy Spirit. The Spirit reveals Jesus to us, He teaches us the knowledge of God and reveals His eternal purpose to us. He comforts us, heals us, and gives us peace and rest. He gives us the faith of Jesus Christ Himself. He empowers us and fills us with joy. He sets us free and fills us with transforming life that is eternal.

Who is this Jesus, this Christ, that we may be made one with and receive all that He is and has? The bible tells us clearly, "He existed before anything was made, and now everything finds completion in Him." Colossians 1:17 (TPT) "For it pleased the Father that in Him all the fullness should dwell, and by Him to reconcile all things to Himself, by Him, whether things on earth or things in heaven, having made peace through the blood of His cross. And you, who once were alienated and enemies in your mind by wicked works, yet now He has reconciled in the body of His flesh through death, to present you holy, and blameless, and above reproach in His sight." Colossians 1:19-22 (NKJV) And again in Colossians 2:9 we read, "For in Him dwells all the fullness of the Godhead bodily." (NKJV)

Take a moment right now to stop and think about some of these statements: everything finds completion in

Christ Jesus; all the fullness of God dwells in Christ Jesus and it pleases the Father; all things (including us) are reconciled to God through Christ Jesus and presented holy and blameless and above reproach. What a hope! And the culmination of this is, "Christ in you, the hope of glory." Colossians 1:27[b] (NKJV)

This is the Jesus we get to be one with! Nothing we feel, think, desire or experience is worth holding onto to keep us from turning and coming to Him, the all-inclusive fullness of God who fills all things and is the center of all things. He is our very own hope of glory! And in all His majesty He meets us here on earth. He makes Himself available to those who seek Him and He desires to be our friend as well. And all that He asks of us is that we come to Him.

Nine

There is an attribute of God, found in Christ, that all humans seek, and that attribute is love. There isn't one among us who doesn't desire to be loved. Some of us have been loved well, some have loved and been loved but something went wrong and it ended. Some have never been loved well. No matter our experience, we all have been created with a desire to be loved and to love.

The Bible says that God is love. "... God is love, and he who abides in love abides in God, and God in him." 1 John 4:16[b] (NKJV) Romans 8:39[b] tells us that for believers nothing "... shall be able to separate us from the love of God which is in Christ Jesus our Lord." (NKJV) His love is eternal and all-inclusive. He doesn't withdraw it for any reason. It never stagnates and it never grows cold. When our hearts turn and we truly come to Jesus we come into love and in oneness, God abides in us. And dear friends, even if we don't turn our hearts and come to Him, He continues to love us. If we don't come to Him, we miss out on knowing true love experientially. Not knowing the pure love of God means we miss out on filling the deepest desire of our hearts with a love that no human expression of love can match.

To go a step further is the issue of loving other people. I struggled for years knowing I really didn't care about most people, let alone love them! I had been emotionally abandoned, rejected, and betrayed and I unconsciously put a shield around my heart to protect myself. I would come to Jesus and confess my lack of love for others and repent because God's Word clearly directs us to love others more than we love ourselves. I would be lifted up by Love Himself and I would feel His compassion and care for me only humbling me more. In His kindness, He took gentle care to not only unwrap the layers I had built and secured over the years but also to heal the wounds that caused me to build them. It took some years because there were layers of protection that started in early childhood. Little by little the Holy Spirit would show me a layer and release me from it.

One day I realized I had been loving others as I never thought I could. That is abiding in Love and letting Love do His work. I still love myself too much and still need more unwrapping and healing but each encounter with the pure love of God is changing me and imparting that pure love into me. I know the place of love and little by little by abiding there, God's love will increasingly be free to flow out of me to others.

This is the simplicity that is in Christ. I came to Him in sincerity with my lack and inability to love others. He lifted me and comforted me in His love and did what was necessary to free my heart to know His love and impart love into my heart for others. All I have to do is to keep coming to Jesus. I love the old hymn, The Love of God. The chorus often comes to my mind refreshing my spirit. "The love of God, how rich and pure! How measureless and strong! It shall forevermore endure the saints' and angels' song." The depth and breadth and width and height of God's love are unfathomable!

Ten

We've seen that all the fullness of God, of the Godhead (Holy Trinity), dwells in Jesus Christ. Knowing this we must agree that no individual one of us can contain all that God is. This fulness will be seen in the true church, the body of Christ.

A large percentage of the church in America has been void of the rich fullness of God found in Christ. That fullness can only be expressed through those who love Jesus above all else, embracing Him always as their first love, and surrendering all to Him. That fullness that brings us into true unity with one another allows God to be expressed on the earth through His people.

There have been many compromises with the world watering down the true gospel. There has been the creation and practice of religious ordinances keeping the life-flow of the Holy Spirit at bay. People have come to the church's doors seeking charismatic speakers and feel-good songs and easy-to-swallow preaching instead of coming to Jesus Christ Himself. Leaders have taken the place of Jesus allowing people to depend upon them instead of teaching them to go to Jesus. Jesus said it all in Rev. 3:20 (NKJV), "Behold, I stand at the door and knock. If anyone hears My voice and opens the door, I will come in to him and dine with him, and he with Me." Jesus is standing at the door of many churches today. He is knocking. Oh, that the doors may be opened to Him.

The book of Revelation begins with the apostle John telling us that this is the Revelation of Jesus Christ and it is written to the churches. Chapters 2 & 3 highlight the problems the church was facing at the time John wrote the book and the problems it would face in the future. First and foremost, they left their first love. They were diligent in works and labor. They were patient and they didn't side with evil. They even persevered without getting weary – all for His name's sake. But somewhere along the way they stopped coming to Jesus to live and move and have their being in Him. They left Him, their first love. May we take heed to the warning. May we run to sit with Jesus day after day. It is only there, in His presence, that love grows and captivates us, abides in us and changes us into His likeness, and holds us in unity and the will of the Father.

Once we leave our first love the doors of the church open to some or all of the offenses to the Lord that follow in these two chapters: false prophets leading God's people into deception, putting idols (things we love and honor more than God) first, sexual immorality, compromise, dead works, pride over what man does, lukewarmness, and spiritual death. In God's eyes, those were standing in pride and were wretched, miserable, poor, blind, and naked. He warns again and again for the churches to have an ear to hear what the Spirit is speaking to us, the church, the body of Christ - the Body meant to contain all the fulness of the Godhead. The Body that glorifies God on earth.

It is clear in each of the seven churches that some stand in Christ, who do not defile themselves, and who hold fast to their first love, Jesus Himself. But Jesus is calling out to all who have come to Him as Savior to take heed, to respond to what the Spirit is speaking so that they will open the door to Jesus only and come to Him day after day.

Eleven

While Jesus was on earth He spoke of the bridegroom. We can read His words in the gospels which tell us that Jesus spoke of the bridegroom being with his friends but one day he would be taken away. He also taught about virgins going out with lamps to meet the bridegroom and warned that only some of these were wise. The wise ones took vessels of oil for their lamps but the foolish did not and while waiting for the bridegroom all rested and slept. In the dark of night, the cry went out that the bridegroom was coming and all the virgins got up to answer the call to go out and meet him. The foolish ones did not have the needed extra oil for their lamps so they had to go out to buy more oil. As they journeyed to make their purchase, the bridegroom came and only the ready virgins went in with him to the wedding and the door was shut. (Matt 25)

John the Baptist was always clear that his calling was to prepare the way for Jesus's ministry. He tells us, "He who has the bride is the bridegroom; but the friend of the bridegroom, who stands and hears him, rejoices greatly because of the bridegroom's voice…" John 3:29[a] (NKJV) Those who develop a life of always coming to Jesus are those who become His friends on this earth. They are those who learn and recognize the sound of His voice. They are those who keep the eternal light burning in their hearts, the vessels of oil, and one day when they hear the bridegroom calling, they will be ready to make the journey to go out to meet Him and to go into the wedding as His bride.

In Revelation 21 John was shown the bride, the Lamb's wife. If you've ever watched a bride who is overcome with love and desire for her bridegroom you probably noticed that as she walked down the aisle her eyes were fixed on him, and his eyes were fixed on her. This is a picture of love I never want to forget. My heart desires to grow into such love for Jesus that I never take my eyes off Him. It is the heart of the virgins Jesus spoke of who waited and looked for Him and were ready to meet Him, their bridegroom.

If we desire to live our life answering Jesus's call to come and if we continue to respond to His call, we will become like Him and truly be one with Him. This is the culmination of our coming to Jesus. This is the maturing of the bride of Christ. In Revelation 22:17 we see the lovers of Jesus, in unison with the Holy Spirit, issue the last call to come to Jesus, "The Spirit and the bride say, 'Come!' And let the one who hears say, 'Come!' Let the one who is thirsty come; and let the one who wishes take the free gift of the water of life." (NIV)

At the end of the book of Revelation John, as the testifier, writes of these words of Jesus, "He who testifies to these things says, 'Surely I am coming quickly'". Revelation 22:20 (NKJV) Jesus is no longer calling but rather is the One who is coming. And John's response is, "Amen. Even so, come, Lord Jesus!" Revelation 2:20[b]

My prayer for all who read this book is that each one will hear the call to come and respond over and over again seeking the face of Jesus. No matter where you stand each day – hungry or not hungry, feeding on the Word or having no taste for it, full of hope or lacking hope, having yet to come for the first time or continuing to come daily – whatever your case may be, the call is to simply *come*. Just come to Jesus in simplicity and honesty and out of living such a life our voices will join with John's as we together respond to the One who is coming.

Even so, Yes! Come, Lord Jesus.

www.ingramcontent.com/pod-product-compliance
Lightning Source LLC
LaVergne TN
LVHW051607080426
835510LV00020B/3173